The First Book of a Seeker

Mahakaal - Secrets of Life

ABHINANDAN DESAI

The First Book of a Seeker

Mahakaal - Secrets of Life

ABHINANDAN DESAI

PAPER TOWNS
PUBLISHERS

PAPER TOWNS
PUBLISHERS

First published by
Papertowns Publishers
72, Vishwanath Dham Colony,
Niwaru Road, Jhotwara,
Jaipur, 302012

The First Book of a Seeker

ISBN Print Book – 978-93- 94670-29- 7

Cover by Neha Agrawal
nehaa.2089@gmail.com

Lord Hanuman

The one who can expand beyond the Universe and shrink as small as an atom.

The one who has all Bramhadnyan without even a glimpse of Ahamkara.

The one who can kill bhayankar Asuras yet the one with eyes full of tears seeing Sita in captivity.

One who is Ajaramar yet a Shunya.

I dedicate this book to you, let everyone become a Shunya.

INTRODUCTION

During the first lockdown of COVID19, and even afterwards, I realized how miserably the world handled the situation just to make business out of it. It was a foolish idea to say that sitting at home will save you from a virus. An organism that is just the size of a particle can penetrate through everywhere. That is what we saw, virus spreading across people sitting at home without any reason.

That is when I realized how much information people are missing about life and its secrets. I gave references of many books & various Gurus I met or learned from to my friends and colleagues, to get good knowledge about life, health, ancient wisdom, etc. However, I observed that people are lazy enough not to do anything for it.

That is when I started writing this book. I am lucky enough to stay with and learn from many great Gurus directly, and indirectly. I am also lucky enough to read so much spiritual fiction, religious literature, and understand the same. My whole spiritual learning journey started because of my sister, Ratan. It is because of her that I met my Gurus, Shri Pranasiddhar & Shri Pranaraj. Many years I spent with them which revealed so many things about life and Maya to me that I cannot pay back this debt to my Gurus.

Later, I also had a chance to meet and learn from Guru Shri Sunil Kale and many more things were revealed then as well.

Various books I read and various lectures of enlightened beings kept me enlightening. I bow to them for such a great work they have done for humanity and this book is just reflection their knowledge in my words.

After writing most of the book, there was a big halt and another trigger came from my friend Anup Kadam, who not only pushed to finish this one, but also triggered the next one of this series.

Surely, the most important support is of my parents, Mrs. Prabha & Mr. Neminath Desai, and my wife Anuja, and my whole family who kept supporting me at every stage of life – credit goes to them and all of the above.

Contents

The Exit of Ram

Wind was blowing high and cold on the huge mountain of Mahashakti, as if some Asura was trying to stop Atri and Aditya who were going to the mountaintop. Today is very important day for all KaalYoddha's (warriors of time & space). They have been waiting for this day for the last 20 years. Therefore, Atri and Aditya started walking very fast on the steep steps of Mahashakti and reached to the top where their Guru, Shri Anantadrishti, was waiting along with his other disciple, Advait.

Ram was sitting on the couch, chatting with his family. His mother, Ankita, was the best mother a child could have, and his father, Ritesh, the best father. They raised their children, Ram and Pooja, in the best way possible. So, on this Sunday evening, they were just having a good family time. They were talking about a very unusual topic for modern families. About Ramayana. They were talking about how Ravan's death also sent Lord Ram into tears, such a kind and compassionate king was Lord Ram. "I will play Lord Ram's character" Pooja said and asked her brother Ram to play Ravan's character. Ram, being her elderly brother, happily agreed, and they started playing the scene of Ravan's death.

"Hey Ravan, on your deathbed, I am feeling sorry for my deeds and yours. Things could have been different if we would have made different choices," said Lord Ram.

"Oh Dearest Lord Ram, I apologize that I couldn't recognize you, the personification of Lord Vishnu. I did not even recognize myself. I was a true Shiva Bhakta (disciple) and I could have been a different person. I have so good karma to support my life but my wrong desires destroyed everything. I apologies for my mistakes, Oh Lord Ram," said Ravan.

Ritesh said in between the scene "Oh, that's a good, detailed statement. Where did you get that?" Ram also thought about it but could not get a clue. "I don't know, it just came into my mind while acting Ravan. Maybe it's the after effect of watching Ramayana".

So, Ram started acting for Ravan's final death scene. With some drama, he showed the pain which Ravan was going through and closed his eyes.

Aditya said to Atri "This is THE time Atri. Pull Ram into Kaalganga (Time River). Advait, you keep Aatmasthan (temporary place for soul stay) ready for Ram's soul. I am guarding the Kaaldwara (door of time dimension) to keep watch on Asuras". Ram's soul entered through the Kaaldwara into Aatmasthan. Anantadrishti cleared out the additional unwanted energies that came with Ram's soul and pushed him into his ashram. He said, "Let Ram remain here till tomorrow morning. His soul will not understand a thing. We will wait till tomorrow to tell him what has happened".

Ankita and Ritesh clapped loudly "Bravo, bravo – what a performance. I am sure you are going to make good actors at least, and earn your bread and butter if you don't like anything else to do in your life". Pooja smiled and sat on the couch again, checking her mobile as it rang in between. She said "Ram, this is enough of acting, now get up. I am hungry and can't wait anymore to eat the special Pulav rice Mom has cooked today". Ram was still lying there on the ground. Ritesh said, "Ram, okay. We agree that you are a better actor. Come, take this award from me". Still there was no response from Ram. Ankita also called "Ram, come on, enough, get up and let us have nice dinner". They did not know what had happened.

Ram did not respond at all. How could he? Ankita, Pooja, Ritesh, all went near him to give him a surprise and shout in his ears, but Ram was not there. How could Ram respond? Now, an Asura of fear started grabbing their minds. They pushed Ram, trying to wake him up. They soon realized something was wrong. Ritesh pushed him vigorously, but upon seeing no response, his mind went numb. Ankita and Pooja started crying, and Ritesh could not figure out what to do. He tried to check Ram's pulse but nothing was ticking inside Ram. They called an ambulance; neighbors came in as well after hearing the loud cry. The Ambulance came in quickly, and everyone rushed to the hospital. Doctor declared natural death of Ram upon inspection.

How in this world was anyone going to believe that? Ram was just 20 years old, a very energetic, active, healthy boy. He was the best Yoga student his teacher had. How could this happen to Ram? Thoughts like these slowly got stirred into the dark night for Ritesh's family. No one had any clue.

Aditya, Atri, and Advait were the best three KaalYoddha's that Anantadrishti had. He had been training them for last 700 years. Time, i.e. Kaal, was never a barrier for any of them, especially when they had Anantadrishti on their side. They had been living in their Guru's ashram on top of the Mahashakti Mountain for past 700 years. No one knew how old the Guru was himself. Mahashakti Mountain remained there for millions of years and had witnessed almost everything in the Universe. This was also the birthplace for Guru Shri Anantadrishti, and hosted their Ashram as well. Mahashakti was surrounded by dense forest with all kinds of wild animals. Trek to the top was something that even the fittest of people would not dare of.

Anantadrishti spent thousands of years to bring Mahashakti to current stage so that it could become KaalYoddha's abode. He created a dense forest around it and brought wild animals so that very few dared to come in. It was almost impossible to climb to the top for any usual person. Moreover, Anantadrishti had kept the ashram in Kaalganga (Time River) so that it was never visible to normal human eyes, airplanes flying nearby, or even to satellites above. Only those who had attained 20 Kaaltantu's (Threads of time and space) were able to locate doors of the ashram and get in.

Anantadrishti had been training KaalYoddha's for thousands of years. They were always on war with Asuras. Anantadrishti took birth on Mahashakti Mountain and he was nothing but Ansh (part) of the Mahakaal (Another dimension of Lord Shiva) and one who could see beyond all Mayas (virtual universe). It was the time when Asuras were on top of their existence and people's minds were heavily corrupted. Mahakaal was beyond Maya in which humans were living. Maya was an illusionary world where this universe was existing. There were several such infinite Mayas, and Mahakaal was controlling each one of them. However, in the Pruthvi Maya, things went different. Mahakaal was keeping everyone's account and was helping the souls to come out of Maya when time comes. Nevertheless, with Asura's influence, things changed drastically. Humans forgot their paths and rode onto the one which was not supposed to be theirs. Therefore, they landed up in untimely exits. All the souls of Pruthvi Maya existed earlier as part of Naag Maya. During their Naag Maya existence, they had higher powers. In Naag Maya, humans could take any form and shape. Thoughts were directly used as medium of conversation, and there was no need for anyone to speak out. Most of the humans in Naag Maya spent their time to do Tapasya (meditation) and Dhyan to attain higher powers. When they attained next level, they used to become Naag Muni; A next level human being, which could control different Mayas and help the usual running of the Mayas. If they do even more Tapasya after being Muni, they become Rhushi. A Rhushi is the ultimate who controls all Mayas. But more than controlling, they were the Rachit, i.e., designers of it. They were the ones who decided how each of the Mayas would unfold. It was them who decided that when a human in Naag Maya performs wrong deeds, their soul would be taken into Pruthvi Maya. They would live a normal life, going through suffering and sorrows and joys and pleasures. They would be under the influence of Maya, and so, of Asura and Sura, too. Asura was an impactful energy, which forced them to do things more aggressively, mainly towards Tamasic Karma, which are called as bad karma as per modern world. Sura also had the same impact but things were more Satvik, i.e., positive karma as per modern world.

This is when a need of warriors came into existence for each of the Maya, and infinite Anantadrishti took birth as Ansh of Mahakaal himself.

Next morning, Ritesh and his family performed the rituals. The whole family, friends and society mourned for Ram's departure. Clueless, they came back home, and in just a few days, all the family members started losing fully on their health. With no clue of how and what happened with Ram, they started losing interest in life, work, and eventually, everything. Relatives and neighbors gossiped about how a happy, healthy family got touched by such rude fate. Nothing was going right with this family.

Entry of the Ultimate Guru

On Mahashakti, though, the next morning after getting Ram there was the brightest and most awaited one. Ram's soul came into senses and could not figure out what had happened. He saw Anantadrishti and his three warriors in front of him. "Who are you? Where am I?" Ram cried loudly. "It is time to ask these questions to yourself, Ram". Anantadrishti said. "You are dead for the mortal world now. We will explain everything, you just be patient with us.

Aditya, you three start imparting Shakti to Ram's soul and once he attains the highest level, let me know," Anantadrishti said. "Ram's family is in great trouble. Asuras of fear and uncertainty have captured their minds. Because of this family, we have Ram with us today. Therefore, it is our duty to re-write some things. I have already created kaalpatals (packages of time & space having specific scenes and memory) that will alter their life," he continued. They showed Ram how his death happened and how his family is suffering with health and finance and the whole world has collapsed for them.

Aditya opened the Kaaldwara and inserted kaalpatals into Ritesh and his family. It was a different scene altogether now..

After Ram got unconscious, Ritesh and family took him to the hospital very calmly. They were sad, but no Asura was able to grab their minds unlike the earlier situation. When the doctor announced Ram's death, they all prayed together and informed all friends and relatives. Rituals were performed. Things remained silent but stable at their home and they slowly came back to their routine lives without any sorrow.

When Ram saw it, he was mesmerized and clueless. "What did you do, and why is my family not mourning for me? I am happy that they are not into any trouble like you showed me earlier, but what is all this?"

Anantadrishti said, "Ram, patience is the key here. We will explain everything. You must first receive the Shakti, and then all answers shall come to you."

Next day, Aditya finished working on Ram and things totally changed for Ram. Ram now had abilities to see everything. Past and Future, Health and Wealth, and what not. He was able to read minds of all living beings. He evolved from being Ram to a cleared Soul. Still, the realization was yet to come.

Anantadrishti came in and checked Ram. "Great work, I don't have to worry about Ram and his capacities to absorb Shakti and Knowledge. Ram, now we will discuss all the questions you have."

Ram said, "What should I call you?" "You can call me Gurushri. All my students call me the same." Gurushri said.

Ram then asked, "Now I know why my family is not mourning. But why did you alter the kaalpatals (time packages)?"

Gurushri said, "We as KaalYoddha have our duties for Humans. We need to help them to go on the right path as well as bring them out of Asura effects when needed."

"Doesn't this change their fate or destiny?" Ram asked.

"No. There is no single fate or destiny. It is always a combination of Karma and desires that can lead to infinite possibilities. Ram, let us go back and see the kaalpatals of your family and what we changed," Gurushri said. This will explain everything, and you will have answers to all your questions.

Ritesh and Ankita were born in the small town of Dronagiri. Ritesh's father, Mukund, was a very famous astrologer. Not a usual one though, people actually saw him as a Spiritual Guru. Mukund's kaalpatals were also changed when Ram's exit happened. Earlier, he was just a good, simple astrologer. Now he was sought as a Spiritual Guru.

Ritesh was around 17 years old when this event happened because of altered kaalpatals. Mukund, according to his yearly plan, went to Gir Jungle to meet his astrologer, Guru Shri Yoginath. Gir's jungle is famous for lions and many wild animals. Mukund was walking through the dense forest when suddenly he realized some changes in the environment. Monkeys were shouting loudly and so were the birds. This was a sign of some big animal nearby, probably a lion. Mukund started walking towards Yoginath's cave very quickly. Before the cave came into sight, something very big jumped on him. He fell on the ground and that thing grabbed his leg. It started dragging him very fast but surprisingly the animal was dragging him towards guru's cave itself. He could not see the animal as the animal had grabbed his legs and was dragging him ferociously. Mukund thought this might be the end now, and started praying to his favorite deity, Lord Hanuman. He knew one thing for sure, whatever you think during your last moments has a big impact on your further Gati (further progress of soul after death). Suddenly, his head hit a rock in between and all lights were out for him.

He woke up after a couple of hours and saw a familiar place. He was in Yoginath's cave. Surprised that he was alive, and that too in his guru's cave, he tried to sit up, but his head was very heavy. He checked and realized that a lot of herbs were applied to his wounds and his hand was fractured. He saw a fire burning at the entry of the cave and a figure sitting there in meditating pose. He tried to open his eyes fully, but could not figure out who or what exactly it was. It was surely not his guru, Yoginath. Who was it, then? He turned around and saw clearly. His entire body shivered and he felt a shock wave going through his spine. He could not believe who he was seeing. It was the Great Lord Hanuman himself. Suddenly, he found himself with abundant energy to get up and walk. He just ran there to his kind Lord Hanuman and fell on his legs. Tears were flowing from his eyes, as if all his karmas had burned away. What a magnificent view that was. Lord Hanuman was almost 15 feet tall, his face and entire body was glowing with so much Teja (divine glow). The whole environment was filled with a sweet fragrance that was originating from Lord himself. His eyes were like a deep cosmic cave, everything was flowing in it. So much of calmness, peace and Ananda (blissful happiness) was in his eyes. As usual,

Lord Hanuman used his magnificent tail to create a circular Aasana (chair), and sat on it.

"I can't express my words, my Lord. Am I dead or really seeing you alive?" Mukund thought he had spoken out loud, but later realized the communication happened only through his thoughts.

"Mukund, you will slowly get used to communicating with thoughts. This means you need to be calm so that you do not think something else which you don't want me to know". Lord Hanuman said with a pleasant smile.

"Mukund, first of all, forgive me for grabbing you and dragging you here. I had to clear out a few of the last karmas left for you as an injury that you suffered just a couple of hours back. This was necessary to give way to your kundalini (the ultimate power, i.e. Shakti that resides in a human as coiled serpent and awakens when the person is ready to receive enlightenment). The shockwave you just felt in your spine was nothing but awakening of this Shakti and flowing upwards while all your tears you just shed now actually cleansed your soul for making a clear path for your kundalini to flow. Now that it is cleansed, I can pass all the knowledge you need to attain for some plans we need you to accomplish. There is a change in cosmic plan and we need to empower you with the Supreme knowledge. It is time to move power from Asuras and distribute to Sura and Humans to balance out the universe, i.e., the Maya we live in," said Lord.

"Was that you, my Lord, who dragged me? That is the reason I did not have fear in mind when that happened."

"Yes Mukund, it was me only. I will now explain you the unknown. You then have to go back and pass this knowledge to the world. Yoginath is none other than me, so I have been guiding you all along the way. I am happy that you followed the right path and now with this knowledge coming to you, you can lead the ultimate path ahead."

Satsangs from Guru – Secrets of Maya & Universe

Ritesh and his mother Radhika were worried. Mukund used to arrive usually in a few days, but it had been a month now. What must have happened to him? "Let Lord Hanuman be with him," Radhika said, unknowingly speaking the reality.

Four more days passed and Mukund returned home. Everyone at home celebrated his return. "Why did it take so long for you to come home? We were so afraid of thinking what had happened to you," Radhika almost yelled at Mukund with tears of joy and worry.

"Ritesh, first you call Ankita, her family, along with all our family members. I want to talk about something very important," Mukund said.

Just in a few minutes, everyone gathered. "Mukund, please tell us now, we cannot hold the suspense anymore," his father said.

Mukund started talking.

"As usual, I went to Gir jungle to meet my Guru Yoginathji. An animal attacked me and I went unconscious while it grabbed and dragged me. When I woke up, it was Lord Hanuman himself sitting there. He told me that we are chosen for a special cosmic cause and we need to be aware of various aspects of the way this world functions, which I will explain to all of you now. My guru is none other than Lord Hanuman himself and he has been waiting for the right time to impart this knowledge," Mukund said.

"Now tell me, what time is it right now? It is almost five in the evening. Now, do you think is it really five in the evening? What we call as time is nothing but perception of our imagination that time is passing. This illusion comes because earth is rotating around self and the sun. Isn't it?

Earth rotates around self; hence, days and nights are there. Earth rotates around the sun; hence we get years of time. Even if you see modern clocks, they are based on oscillations/radiation frequency of cesium atom. This means, it is eventually based on the electrons rotating around the nucleus and giving illusion of some movement that we assume as time."

Everyone at home wondered how easily they were able to understand this, even without any background education.

Mukund continued. "So, time is nothing but an illusion created because of something that is rotating around self or other. So, in absolute terms, there is nothing called as time. Time is just an illusion or perception," Mukund said.

Surprisingly, one question came into Ritesh's mind. "Father, how can it be an illusion? I see myself and everyone getting older, I can imagine what has happened in the past but cannot go back there. I go to different places and can really feel that time is passing."

"Bang on. That is the right question, my son. You get an illusion of time passing because of the space you live in. You move around in this space and so does the earth, sun, atoms, or electrons. Therefore, the illusion of time comes only on the basis of existence of space. If there were no space, there would not have been time. Therefore, space and movements combined give an illusion of time because of atomic to cosmic level movements and rotations happening.

However, if we talk about space, do we really know what space is? Space, as we see, is present in between us, in our house, on and around earth, and so, in the whole universe. Do you think the space is really infinite or is it also just an illusion? Meaning of the word Shiva (Shi+Va) itself is Shi, i.e., Stillness where of all movement, i.e., Va is born. Lord Shiva once said to Saptarishi (The first seven sages who learned about cosmic knowledge, i.e. Brahmadnyan from Lord Shiva himself) on the question of size of the universe that he could fit the whole universe on to the space present on the speck of dust. Moreover, if we want, we can expand it to infinite limits. Space is void, a stillness, and it does not have a size. It can be a Bindu (dot), as well as infinite. Therefore, what we call as space is a void thought of absolute Brahman or the cosmic soul, and big bang is just like an initiation of energies (Shakti) into this void emerged because of the thought of this Brahman. These energies then take different forms in this absolute void as matter and life. However, eventually it is nothing but a void. It is what is called as Maya, i.e. combination of Shiva and Shakti, i.e. stillness imparted with movements. It is called Duality or Dvaita. Hence, we call something that is beyond this Maya as Advaita, i.e., which is non-duality, which is The One. It is attribute less, i.e., Nirguna and Nirakar. When one transcends from Advaita to Dvaita, we think or perceive that as reality because it gets dimensions," Mukund said.

"Then this means everything is just illusion, father?" Ritesh asked.

"Yes, absolutely. Hence, it is called as Maya (illusion). Maya is nothing but the projection of energies/movement onto kaalpatals (i.e., time and space together impregnated with energies) and it creates illusion of the world that we see. In this illusionary world that we live in, or we rather think we live in; everything is guided by karma and desires. The energies, which are projected on kaalpatals, are nothing but Shiva and Shakti. Therefore, it is like an illusionary tube or conduit on which combinations of Shiva and Shakti are together projected. Every soul that sees this projection believes as if it is living all those infinite combinations of pre-recorded scenes based on the soul's karma and desires. How that happens we will see tomorrow morning," said Mukund with a pleasant but naughty smile. They all had dinner together and slept.

Next morning, after breakfast, everyone gathered again. It was not much of an issue to digest the knowledge obtained last night for everyone with the blessings of lord Hanuman. When the time comes, supreme knowledge is very easy to digest, and when it is not the right time, no matter how hard one tries, their karma will only block the access to such supremacy. They were unable to control the eagerness to learn more. They now surely knew, as Mukund said, they were chosen for something special and every moment of time became very interesting for them, as if time was really real for them.

Even before Mukund could start, Ankita asked a question this time "Uncle, if everything is Maya, i.e., an illusion, then why are we here? Who are we?"

Mukund said, "See, your questions mark the exact next stage of our talks. We know the fact that we are just a body, i.e., an accumulation of five elements (Earth, Water, Fire, Air and Space) with energy, i.e., Prana and embodiment of thought of Brahman, i.e., our Soul. It is all about the soul, that brings karma with it, while body and its mind function based on the karma & karmic memory. Along with desires, they define the future path. As I said, the whole world is Maya; there is not a single Maya. Let us call for a simplification that Maya is one universe. Therefore, there are infinite universes, i.e., Maya, around there and each Maya is a thought of absolute Brahman with its own space and time dimensions.

Each Maya is nothing but a mesh of time and space threads, which we can call as Kaalpatals. The whole universe of Maya is a mesh of a single Kaaltantu crossing itself in infinite places and loops, thus creating a mesh around. It does not have specific number of dimensions as it is absolutely void when you look from outside. However, when inside, it is purely based on time and space. As awareness of one increases, more dimensions are opened for him/her and eventually when awareness is full, one understands that it is all void and that is what we call as enlightenment.

We live in Pruthvi Maya as Humans. Of course, we have thousands of other animal species here. We all come here as a learning and punishment for our souls which are originated from another Maya. Each soul that comes has to go through all these species or Yonis taking rebirth each time, eventually to get a birth of human where one has power of mind and thoughts and emotions unlike lower Yonis.

Our souls come from Naag Maya. Each body (human or animal), by birth, based on their punishment and learning needs, gets access to several Kaaltantu's (time and space threads of a kaalpatals). All humans are having access to minimum of 10 Kaaltantu's. Below that, it is animal kingdom and they were mainly living with their Vasana's, i.e., tendencies, and there is not much of scope of thought process. Humans, on the other hand, with more Kaaltantu's are able to make choices on what exactly they want ahead.

At birth itself, when souls come from Naag Maya, they are handed over a character to play and Kaaltantu's they can hold. They could have anything between 10 to 20 Kaaltantu's. The more they have it, the better they can live, as there is more clarity of thoughts and choices. More Kaaltantu's mean they can simply make better choice of road ahead and not get stuck into the Maya, nor under influence of Sura-Asura. Once they start playing the characters on Pruthvi, they tend to forget their source and remain under influence of Maya and Sura/Asura.

Humans then usually live the life based on the karma their soul brings and desires that arise from their character. For each possible combination of karma and desire, there are infinite ways a human can live a life. All these are present in the complex mesh of time and space which modern world people call as parallel worlds. It's a human choice based on desires, karma, and Sadsadvivekbuddhi (wisdom that helps to choose right path or to do the right action) which then decides which Kaaltantu's will be accessed for this logical choice. As example, suppose we are sitting here and talking, and our conversation drifts into disagreement. We might then depart this life with grudge and hatred in mind. That is one Kaaltantu. Or we can talk sweetly, like this, wherein you understand how the universe functions and we lead to a very simple, mature life altogether, with the understanding of how we can make it better. This is another Kaaltantu. So, such infinite possible combinations are already there in the mesh and it is up to us which one to choose. The situation is not so easy every time. Karma, desires & Runanubandha (attachments with different souls and combined karmas of souls), along with Sura/Asura, can play deadly games with characters. Runanubandha is also a very interesting concept. When a soul takes birth, it takes birth based on its Sanchit karma (main store of karma which soul has to go through) and chooses only a part of it which can be taken to this life called as Prarabdha karma (part of main karma base for soul which it took to go through in this life). Now if Runanubandha was not there, there are hundreds of parents having the same karmic combinations where a soul can take birth and live those chosen karma. But it is Runanubandha which decides that this soul has to live the chosen karma with specific set of souls which are nothing but family, relatives, friends, and all people that the soul meets in current life. That is why we are so tightly tied together with Runanubandha that no soul can escape it. People often think that as an example, after marriage, they continually fight with their spouse and for no reasons their life just becomes miserable. This is nothing but a repay and replay of your karma which you did in earlier lives with the other souls which have become your family or friends now and you all have to suffer or enjoy those karmas together. Hence, in Bharat (India), there is a tradition to become Sanyasi (Hermit), i.e., to renounce all the Runanubandha one has and lead to a lone life where karmas will unfold in a totally different way. Lot of people try to become Sanyasi but they are unware of the fact that if they leave the Runanubandha so directly, they have to go through a lot of suffering to remove those karmas which they were supposed to suffer with their family or friends. They move back to their normal life thinking that becoming Sanyasi is the most difficult thing. It is surely the most difficult thing but one should opt this path only when someone has the right level of awareness and a true Guru to guide.

Understand Role of Gods

Let us take a detailed example now of how different combinations of scenes get chosen based on desires and actions. Imagine a situation where one rich man who needs to suffer for one of his past deeds of cheating his business partner in earlier life, is going on a leisure trip with his current family. During the trip, the travel agency person cheats on them and takes away all their money & belongings. Now this family is in big trouble, they are in a deserted place with no help to arrive. This man's wife suffered a lot of domestic violence in earlier life. After waiting there for some time, they started quarreling around whose fault this is. During that quarrel, the man started hitting his wife (which he regularly does in this life as well). Seeing that, his son and daughter who were still calm, started feeling sad and angry. This situation gets worse as Asuras of fear and death and uncertainty started grabbing their minds. Now as the man started hitting his wife even harder, their son's mind is grabbed fully by an Asura and he goes ahead and pushes his father. The Man then falls down on the rock and bleeds to death. The son, then runs away and grows as a Gangster while the wife and daughter become low class labors because the remaining wealth of the man is also taken over by his partners.

This sounds like a typical story of a movie, and unfortunately, there is no savior or Hero here, as there is no fixed story in a cosmic movie".

"Then does this mean we don't have any control over what happens even if we have more Kaaltantu's?" Ankita asked sadly.

Mukund said, "No, it's not about controlling what is going to happen. It's about letting the things happen based on karma and past memory, but wisdom is to choose that Kaaltantu which still leads to the best possible combination of situations in life"

"How can a normal human, who doesn't even know about these concepts choose Kaaltantu?" Ritesh asked.

"The key is awareness and Sadsadvivekbuddhi. Hence, if you see, the whole Indian traditional education was based on concepts to increase and manage Sadsadvivekbuddhi to handle life better than handling just business or job. Let me now tell you if, in the earlier story that we heard, everyone had awareness, then what could have happened." The story goes something like this now.

During the trip, the travel agency person cheats on them and takes away all their money & belongings. Now the family is in big trouble, they are in a deserted place with no help to come. The Asuras of fear and uncertainty start grabbing their minds. However, with awareness of the situation, they all come together. The man says the road on which we came had a police station a few miles away from here. It is getting dark and we all cannot walk that fast. Therefore, son, if you could go to the police station alone, I will stay with your mother and sister and protect them. You can bring back the police and rescue all of us. The son, who was a very athletic boy, runs towards the police station and brings back the police. Even though they never got that money back, their lives run fine. They reach back home and lead a usual life ahead"

"But, uncle, is it so simple, then, just to stay calm and say everything that happened was because of past karma, and go ahead. Shouldn't that travel agency person get punished"? Ankita said.

"No Ankita, it's not our worry to handle or punish wrong deeds of others. As I mentioned, the Kaalpatals consist of all possible combinations, and if everyone is aware, the Maya runs in Satyug, i.e., age of truth, i.e., everyone chooses the best Kaaltantu and leads best lives. As the awareness goes down and down, we go through Tretayug and Dwaparyuga (ancient Vedic terminology of human ages) and when awareness is at the lowest, we call it as Kaliyuga, which is nothing but chaos. At a particular moment of illusionary time, all these Yuga's exist and run in Maya but based on who chooses what, their characters keep on moving from chaotic life to ideal life," Mukund said.

"Father, then what is the role of Gods? Why do we need them?" Ritesh asked.

Mukund answered very calmly "Why do we need them is a very wrong question. We do not need them if awareness is there because when it is there, human itself is a god. You know our ancient saying, right? 'Aham Brahmasmi' i.e. I am the cosmos and so the cosmos is me. This simply means, what is inside is outside, too, and everything is emerged from the same energy. Humans have simply lost awareness of this simple sutra of life (sutra - solution). This has led to diseases like cancer, because each cell of body still knows this information and it simply can't' digest so much hatred or selfishness filled in the human mind, and so it functions wildly and stops performing its duties which we then call as a cancerous cell.

Besides this, gods are celestial souls which are imparted with specific energies and purposes to continue the functioning of all Maya's. As we know, humans can be made aware by different ways, and ancient scriptures have noted them down as Bhakti Marg, Yog Marg, Karma Marg, Dnyan Marg (Wisdom & Knowledge way) etc. (Marg = way, path). A Usual human goes by default with karma Marg and keeps living life by burning karma. This way can be enhanced with awareness of Karma and Maya to bring better options and desires to life. Those who love god can leave everything to their favorite deity and that deity will take care of choosing best Kaaltantu's for their beloved devotee based on how much trust & love is poured in. Remember it is important, it is based on love and trust of devotee and not the exchange offers people offer to God, such as 'you do this and I do that.' Yog Marg is like giving techniques to achieve liberation which, if followed, will bring awareness, bhakti, and karma cleansing automatically. Dnyan marg is for the brilliant ones who study, read and understand everything. That way, they attain all the required knowledge and proceed ahead. The issue with this marg is that many times, this knowledge goes into people's heads and they get diverted from the path.

Usually, when they succeed in any one of the above marg, they can get a natural exit, i.e., death. Of course, based on karma, if any more learning, i.e. Sanchita Karma, is left for the soul in Pruthvi maya, recalculations happen and the soul enters into Maya again, choosing the right time and space in Kaalpatal, taking re-birth. Humans did not know that even 6 months before the time of death, Mahakaal himself starts creating situations wherein the soul slowly moves towards the exit, i.e., death. This is in natural case but with Asura's effect, humans tend to move towards those karmas which cause huge distortions and distractions in their physical and energy bodies. This, then, causes situations like critical or auto-immune diseases, accidents, etc. This is an untimely exit, and the learning which Naag Maya soul was supposed to do here in Pruthvi Maya doesn't happen. Moreover, additional karma also gets loaded for that soul and thus, the soul is trapped almost forever unless a Guru pitches in.

Let us talk about our earlier example again and see how gods can play with Maya. To answer your question, this is the reason they are here, and hence, are important to keep Maya functioning. Because it's not easy for all humans to have greater awareness all the time. They keep falling into situations and lead to outcomes they didn't want.

During the trip, the travel agency person cheats on them and takes away all their money & belongings. Now the family is in big trouble, they are in a deserted place with no help to arrive. Now, after some time, they started quarreling around whose fault this is. During that quarrel, the man starts hitting his wife (which he regularly does in this life as well). Seeing that, his son and daughter who were still calm, started feeling sad and angry. This situation gets worse as Asuras of fear, death and uncertainty start grabbing their minds. Now the son is a devotee of Lord Hanuman. And when Hanuman sees this situation, he jumps in for help. He sends one wolf from nearby jungle to this place. Seeing the wolf, the man and wife come back to senses. Everyone climbs on a nearby tree. The wolf sits there all night and the whole family stays there, empty stomach, shivering in cold. The next morning, a transport truck driver rescues them. They all then go home. Their differences grow over time and the couple gets divorce by the time the kids start their jobs. Kids do well in the rest of their life. Not the best, but they do well.

Therefore, you see, in this case, just because of the son's devotion to one of the Gods, the situation was handled in a much better way. Of course, they did not lead the best life, but this is far better than the first outcome we saw, and this can happen only with interference from the Gods. Life keeps changing the track based on chosen Kaaltantu's, and hence there is no fixed story, even if everything is pre-recorded. Therefore, it is important to remember that no matter what your Prarabdha karma is or what life you are leading, the right awareness, true devotion to God, and patience, will ensure that you lead a good life.

One needs to know that even a small devotion to cosmic energy or God, whatever one calls it, helps humans in every situation. We just do not see the help offered, and the minds grabbed with asuras lead to those Kaaltantu's leading a miserable life". Mukund's father promptly asked, "Mukund, does this mean Karma has no role to play and it is all based on our choices and awareness?"

Mukund replied "No, father. As I said already, every situation in life that a human faces, is based on karma only. It is Karma that decides which part of kaalpatals you will be in, i.e., simply speaking, what situation you will face. But then, karma can only create a situation but cannot decide how it will unfold. It is desires and awareness levels that lead to the next situation. The next situation will be on better side if awareness is higher, and Vice Versa."

Ram said to Anantadrishti "This is the Brahmadnyan, the supreme knowledge. Why is it not told to everyone then?"

Anantadrishti replied, "Ram, it's been given to humans from time to time. How many of them really understand and implement it is again based on their awareness. Modern Humans try to bring everything to a logical conclusion but that is not how real cosmos works. When you use bindu sharir (body that can be used to do so called time travel) and come out of kaalpatals and Maya, you see that everything is just standstill. There is nothing moving in this world. Souls ride the time and space Maya situations to lead to another situation from the current one. During this, they either burn their karma and finish learning if awareness is high, or they just get more trapped into the Maya and never come out."

Karma & Desire – Wisdom of Rhushis

"But if karma can decide only the situation you are currently in, then the next situation should also be decided by Karma only," Mukund's father said again.

"No, father. Even though it is true in a sense, it cannot decide what is going to happen next. Karma can just create a situation. How the situation then unfolds fully depends on the desires and actions happening in that scene. In astrology, if you remember, only that Pandit is good who can not only tell what has happened to you in the past or what is going to happen in the future, but also what needs to be done to be on the right path if something happens. There are very few like this on earth because the rest just read the karmic calculations and predict what could happen, i.e., they only calculate how the situation will be created in your life. They cannot predict how it will unfold once you enter that situation. But the real Pandits can also see the soul's purpose, i.e., for what learnings the soul came into Pruthvi Maya, based on which its karmas are recorded. Accordingly, then the Pandit can guide that person so that the scenes in their life unfold exactly or similarly to how they wish, with less harm.

Our great Rhushi Agasti was the first one to understand and note this. He is a great, enlightened energy soul. He just went into a void, i.e., from where you actually see the standstill world and all static scene combinations. He observed it neatly, then, and analyzed the full mesh of Kaalpatals. Then he added maths (Sankhya) and planet positions into it and created Nadi reading scriptures for astrological predictions (scriptures present in Bharat, i.e., India, which can read out past and future of any human). Remember, Sankhya Shastra (ancient Indian science of math and numbers) is the base for everything. Everything in this universe can be represented by Sankhya Shastra. It is the base of everything that we know. Therefore, such great Rhushi Agasti created these Nadi reading scriptures, which can tell the past and future of any character. But wisdom is to understand how situations will unfold based on the character's desires and awareness. Now, as time passed, these scriptures have gone and very few have the real but partial scriptures. Hence, people do not believe in Nadi reading, nor in astrology. It is a part of Kaliyuga effect anyways. A good astrologer should be able to see what situation a person is going to go through, based on their karma. But then, that is not a fixed story as we said, hence, predictions fail most of the times. Because based on desires and awareness, the story keeps changing and there is no single destiny or fate for a person.

Nonetheless, what I mean here is, karma is the base of all pre-recorded scenes of kaalpatals. However, as souls have come here to learn of their deeds from Naag Maya, they are supposed to have desires. Otherwise, how could the learning happen. There will be no play of Maya without desires. Desires are the base of this whole play of Maya.

Let us learn one example to understand this. Assume a man who has this awareness of Maya, Karma & Desires, decides he will never get angry. He thinks he has understood everything. One day he goes to market with his son. His son's mind is grabbed by a Sura this time, which simply had a wish to eat lots of sweets.

One must understand that Suras and Asuras both are not good for a human mind. Excess of any extreme is dangerous.

So, this man's son starts crying for sweets in the middle of the market. Now the man gets angry, but fortunately remembers that he is not supposed to get angry. Good that the awareness still ticked in his mind. Therefore, he tries to calm his son stating that sweets are not good for his health, etc. Now an Asura takes benefit from this situation and grabs the sweet shop owner's mind. Owner starts to think what rubbish this man is talking. If people hear that they will also think that sweets are not good. I prepare my sweets so carefully and with best material, and thus, the Asura of anger fully grabs the situation. This shop owner now starts arguing with our man about his false allegations. Surprised with the sudden entry of the shop owner, our man forgets about his awareness and starts fighting with him. Their fight turns bad eventually, and the situation leads to those Kaaltantus which would not have come if our man would have stayed aware.

Therefore, in the above case, it was the man's desire not to get angry, while the shop owner's desire was to keep his future and business fine. The kid just had an imposed desire. Now this is an interesting concept called imposed desire. Not all desires arising in a particular situation belong to the character or soul. They might be imposed by Maya, i.e., Sura/Asura or from the situation itself," Mukund said.

Radhika asked a question first time "Then how do we identify which is my desire and which one is imposed?"

Mukund continued, "Yes, that is the reason and base for all religions, ways of living, or ways of enlightenment. As it is so difficult to identify this, great enlightened souls have been guiding humans on simple ways to live life which are nothing but Dharma (Religion). In a simple way, Indians used to opt for Sannyasa (state of moving away from material world for self-realization) only for this reason. Because, for a normal human, it is almost impossible to identify the source of desires. The simplest way was to abandon all desires. But that is a very difficult way, and also not the best way because then your Runanubandha (Sanskrit term to mention karmic relations between souls/characters which can be blood or non-blood relations) remains incomplete. As an example, I have Runanubandha with my parents, with my wife and my kids. We have specific karmas and learnings which tie us together. If I move away from everything, I create a hole in the Kaalpatals and you all might lead to unwished Kaaltantus without my character. I am not saying taking Sanyasa is wrong, but it creates such hollows which then are often taken over by Asura/Sura. It needs proper guidance from a Guru so that such holes are not created and no one ends up in problems because of this.

When Lord Hanuman explained these things to me, he gave a very simple solution to this. He said, why to bother if desire is born from soul or character or sura/asura/maya/situation. When a desire is there, that means it leads to a specific Kaaltantu. Now when you start thinking too much as a normal human about desires and whether to fulfil them or not, you unnecessarily get trapped by asuras of complexity and madness. Desires arise because of character's ego and that ego leads to unwanted or wanted both type of situations. Hence, a simple way to enlightenment was to surrender to your favorite Deity so that there is no ego in you and whatever happens in life you just let it happen and let your deity glide you through it like a feather. Unaffected by everything that happens with eternal devotion and love you are drawn in, life becomes so easy and smooth.

Let us again take the example of our man who desires not to get angry and see how it unfolds now.

So, the man's son asks for sweets. The man knows that his son, being just 5-year-old, wishes for anything that is lucrative. The key here is to either just give him one sweet and take him away from the shop or divert his attention to the fruit stall where mangoes are kept. Now the mangoes were very costly compared to the cost of sweets. One sweet doesn't hurt anyone. It was important to just glide through the situation with minimal impact. So, he buys the sweet, while praising the shop owner on how good his sweets are. When he comes out of the shop, his son is very happy. During his happy state, the man then explains benefits of fruits and creates some story on how eating fruits benefitted a man with good health more than the other who ate junk food.

Therefore, the key to blissful living is awareness and just letting the things flow as smoothly as possible. Now the Rhushis who had all the wisdom and knowledge came up with various methods and techniques for this. For health, they came up with Ayurveda, Siddha Ayurveda, etc. For having the best connection between body, mind and soul, they came up with Yog (Yoga as it is termed in today's world). For wisdom, they came up with great epics like Ramayana, Mahabharata. For explaining about Maya and everything, Vedas and Sankhya, Upanishads and many more scriptures were written. All these give humans the best possible ways to lead a life. Let us understand them one by one.

As I mentioned, everything in this universe started from the thought of cosmic soul and it initiated itself in the form of sound energies first. That is where the sound of Aum was discovered by our great sages. Then these sound energies get converted into matter and eventually into the actual life. Thus, every life or matter has a specific energy pattern at base. When life vibrates itself with cosmic frequency, it just eventually merges into the cosmic frequency. When human vibrates in this same way, we say realization, enlightenment, or liberation happened.

Rhushis learned all this from Shiva, and as I said, came up with all knowledge to us. The most important part for a life to sustain is health. Rhushis came up with Ayurveda wherein they found the base energy pattern of each plant as well as learned how humans and animals have varying energy patterns. Unlike plants where there are no desires or karma or emotions, humans and animals vary their energies based on emotions, karma and desires. When imbalance in energies happen for a human, we call it a disease or sickness. So Rhushis simply termed specific plants for specific health issues based on what health issue is associated with what energy distortion and corruption has happened and which plant can restore it. In addition, they also identified these energy patterns with Vaat, Pitta, Kafa base along with 20 qualities i.e. Gunas of each of them. Based on these qualities and lifestyle of the person, Ayurvedic Vaidya can refer right cure for any health issues present or known. Therefore, Ayurveda has a holistic, deep-rooted philosophy to heal humans unlike modern medicine which does not understand anything about universe or Maya or energy. Moreover, it distorts health completely for untimely exit, i.e., death, instead of healing the person. Siddha & Ayurveda go further steps ahead and talk about Rasayana (technically chemicals, but Rasayana is something that rejuvenates human to restore Shuddha Deham, i.e., perfectly healthy body). They talk about metals and plants and milk and that everything when taken in combination brings humans to a perfectly healthy state. As an example, as per modern world, mercury is poison but Siddha Ayurveda uses it as medicine. We have to remember; modern medicine and science understands each substance by dissecting it into granular substances and then defining their properties. It simply forgets that everything has a base energy pattern, and when things are taken in combination, they behave differently than when taken alone. So, this dissection logic can never help modern scientists to understand healing properties of something unless they learn the ancient ways or the holistic ways. Slowly, the world is moving in that direction wherein they are studying quantum physics and newer sciences which is unfolding greater knowledge. However, it is a very difficult way to learn about cosmos. Modern science wants the Ayurvedic doctors to prescribe the medicine with dissected attribute contents of the herbs. They also want these doctors to limit some contents based on modern ways. This is totally wrong because it removes the holistic and energy-based approach to heal and we then concentrate only on attributes of dissected contents and their abilities to suppress symptoms of diseases rather than healing the body.

Rhushis also established good food habits. Maya has a basic rule, that for a life to sustain, it has to consume life. When we go to the subtle meaning of this, cosmic energy is needed for any life to sustain itself. When food is consumed, the converted form of cosmic energy, i.e., life, is consumed. Key is to keep the conversion form simplest. I.e. Plant life is best for consumption as it sustains itself in very basic form and hence, when consumed, can bring more Satva into life, i.e., Satvik life (life dominated by pure positiveness). The higher the conversion is, i.e., animal life, it brings more Tamas into life, i.e., Tamasic life (life dominated by pure negativity). Hence, if you observe, in spiritual practices, more stress is given to eat only plant-based food, skipping animal-based food. There are spiritual practices such as Aghora, i.e., left hand of the main path, wherein these rules apply differently, but one must understand that these are very different spiritual practices not created for normal human beings. Drinking Madya, i.e., liquor, is a bad habit people have taken from here only. In Aghora, there is a vidhi, i.e., ritual called as Panchamkara which involves 5 Ms; Madya, Maans, Matsya, Mudra & Maithuna, i.e., Liquor, Meat, Fish, Parched Grain & Sex. Aghori (a person who follows Aghora path) performs this ritual with a fresh human corpse in Smashan (crematory) and consumes all above 5 Ms to reach to a different spiritual energy level and to impress the deities. But if you see, today's humans have just stuck to the etheric meaning of this, i.e., they consume liquor, meat, fish and parched grains like anything, increasing the Tamas to very high level. They do not even understand how badly it is affecting their health and mind. They give examples of ancient scriptures where Gods also drink Madira or Somras, but they have forgotten that Somras was nothing but Amrut and it used to bring them into ecstasy with cosmic energy which people have misunderstood as a drunken state. Madira, especially, has curse of all three gods, i.e., Brahma, Vishnu & Mahesh (Three main Gods as per ancient Indian terminology) that whoever drinks it, goes into such deep influence of Maya, it almost becomes impossible to come out of it. In an esoteric way, it actually meant as the one who drinks divine nectar dropping out of penal gland along with Mudra's, done in combination with Yoga and Pranayama, and the one who controls all the desires and thus allows union of Shiva and Shakti inside, can attain the ultimate."

Ritesh asked, interrupting "But father, so many people eat animal-based food, i.e., non-vegetarian, does this mean everyone is Tamasic?"

Mukund laughed and said "Yes and No. Both the answers apply here. Yes, because when they consume animal life, they also consume their emotions and energies. This brings many distortions into their own energies and life. It does not only take too much time to digest and consume, but also distorts system in a bad way. Especially the emotions animals have when they are near death are fearsome. These emotions eventually create Tamas, anger, sadness, and lot of health issues causing untimely death."

"But uncle," Ankita interrupted now, "if a person has good awareness of all this knowledge, then he will find ways to come to normal state and health."

Mukund again laughed out loud and said "Ankita, this is where things go wrong. Knowledge brings awareness in general, but for those who are already Tamasic, it brings more ego. Combination of knowledge and Tamas is ideal example of Rakshas or Asura, because it creates ego. While combination of knowledge and Satva is an ideal example of Deva because it creates wisdom. If you see, all of Rakshasas and Asuras were best in Tapasya (Penance). They did Tapasya for thousands of years with dedication and received boons from the gods. However, you see they ended up being more Tamasic, greedy and lustful. Similarly, lot of people think eating animal life will give them good health but they don't understand their minds are grabbed by Asuras which makes them more egoistic and Tamasic in this birth or next. So, wisdom is to consume plant life as long as possible to avoid any distortions."

"So, just eating plants keeps life simple, and one can attain liberation easily," Radhika said.

"Yes, but that takes millions of years. As souls are trapped with enormous amount of karma, food just becomes a way to stay alive when it comes to liberation. This is the reason that Rhushis also brought up Yog. Yog opens up faster ways to achieve the best health, mind, and soul, thus allowing more open access to cosmic energy, ability to resonate with cosmic frequency, and eventually achieve liberation and self-realization. Modern society thinks of Yog as twisting of body parts. But they have forgotten that everything is energy and when you breathe in specific ways or chant mantras or meditate on Guna or Nirguna aspects of the god, you achieve the ultimate (i.e., attribute form and attribute-less form of almighty). As I said, the phrase Aham Brahmasmi, i.e., I am the cosmos and the cosmos is me, your body which is basically created of physical body, energy body, auric body and bindu sharir, can be used to reach the ultimate state. Moreover, if you add mantras which are nothing but combination of Sanskrit Bij mantra (seed sound), then you can enlighten yourself. Sanskrit is not just a language. Rhushis studied all sound patterns and energy patterns in the universe and noted every base pattern as a letter. These base patterns are also Bij (Seed) mantras which are associated with various cosmic energies as well as Pancha-Mahabhoota, i.e., the five elements which are Pruthvi

(Earth), Jal (Water), Agni (Fire), Vayu (Air) & Akash (Space). Hence, every word in Sanskrit actually exhibits the energy pattern of the situation/thing about which that word explains. In the same way, names of gods/deities also exhibit their specific energy and hence chanting mantras, or god's names, oscillates the human body to that higher energy frequency. Sound, i.e., Naad, is the base of all and if it is used perfectly, then it can lead a person to the ultimate. Again, people have forgotten Sanskrit and its importance and preference given to foreign languages. English, or many other languages, are the most imperfect languages as they don't understand anything about a sound, its associated energy and its effects when it's uttered. Moreover, English does not even have the same pronunciation for one letter every time. This is leading to an era wherein people who actually learn and practice English or any other modern language do not remain so clear in terms of life energy when it was being used in Sanskrit. I agree that most of the Indian or Asian or even a few of the western languages are very similar to Sanskrit, but except from those which are derived from Sanskrit, rest of them might not be so deep rooted to understand about each sound and energy pattern."

Story of Ram

Ram said to Anantadrishti "Gurushri, I understand so many things now. From one perspective, it's very easy to understand how to live a simple life, but from another perspective, there is so much knowledge that a normal human can't grab everything."

Anantadrishti said, "Yes, it is the play of Maya. Let it remain as it is. Souls need to complete their learnings. When they attain a certain level, whichever human character they are playing automatically gets a Guru, either as a real Guru, or knowledge which can come from any means."

Ram now asked with bit of hesitation "Gurushri, what is my role, then? Why did my character receive an untimely exit?"

Gurushri laughed, "Do you think yours is an untimely exit? Your exit is the liberation point for our Maya. Your exit is the most sophisticatedly planned exit, Ram."

Ram could not control now "Please Gurushri, I pray to you, please explain to me my role."

Gurushri said "Yes, Ram. This is the time for self-realization for your soul.

If we talk in Pruthvi Maya's timelines, this started around seventy million years back. Everything in all Mayas was being executed in the right way. Guru Rakshit, who was guru of Asuras, had a big plan. He created an Asura named Kaalahar. Kaalahar was a devotee of Lord Shiva and he spent thousands of years in Tapasya (penance) and asked Shiva two boons. First was to give him powers to kill Mahakaal, and second was to allow him to take Mahakaal's place." Lord Shiva, as you know, is Bholenath, and is always in control of his Bhakts (devotees); he granted him a boon but with conditions."

Kaalahar asked Lord Shiva "My lord, please grant me a boon to kill (Vinaash) Mahakaal and I should be in charge of his place." Lord Shiva smiled and said "Kaalahar, no one can change the basic rules of the universe. Everything and everyone has their role and even we Tridev (Three Gods as Brahma, Vishnu and Shiva) can't change it".

"I want to become immortal and control everyone's life, including entry and exit. This is the boon I seek. You are the Trikaal Dnyani (one who has knowledge of past, present and future) so you decide how I can get my boon," Kaalahar said.

"You wish to have Vinaash (destruction) of Mahakaal. That boon I can grant. But you cannot be immortal. Everything that begins has an end or transformation in this universe. So, you have to accept and respect that fact," Lord Shiva said.

"Then, my dear lord, grant me the boon that only Mahakaal can kill me," Kaalahar said. He was proudly thinking of his own brilliance. Once I kill Mahakaal, how is he going to kill me again?

Lord Shiva smiled.

Everything seemed like it had paused. Mahakaal was watching this conversation. He smiled, too, and immediately gave birth to Anantadrishti so that even when Kaalahar destroys Mahakaal, KaalYoddhas can help run Mayas smoothly.

Lord Shiva was also present with Mahakaal at the time when Anantadrishti took birth. Anantadrishti, being a cosmic child, looked like a half-aged man and just like a Rhushi. He asked "My Lord and dear Father, I am blessed to be your son and a KaalYoddha. I shall remain in my duty whatever you assign to me." Mahakaal said, "Ananta, my son, we both will explain to you the plan. You will remain the KaalYoddha and help human race to evolve. Help individual human beings who possess good qualities. You will come to know when your play will end at the right time. Till then, perform your duties the right way". "Bless you," said both Mahakaal and Lord Shiva.

Kaalahar was feeling very happy inside, thinking how clever he is. He fooled Lord Shiva with two boons as "Allow destroying Mahakaal and I shall be killed by Mahakaal only." He was so happy, thinking once he kills Mahakaal, there is no one who can kill him and thus he becomes immortal and can rule world for infinity."

Lord Shiva said to Kaalahar "Tathastu (let it be as asked). Let you be blessed with what you have wished for." Then he summoned Mahakaal to appear in Pruthvi Maya in front of them. Lord Mahakaal appeared. He bowed to Lord Shiva and stood in front of Kaalahar. Kaalahar bowed to Lord Shiva and with one clean stroke of his sword, he killed Mahakaal. Lord Shiva blessed Kaalahar again and vanished into air.

All gods from Swarglok (Heaven) were watching this. They went furious. This is what always happens. An Asura does the penance and Lord Shiva grants him a boon. Then he rules the universe and we suffer. This time Lord Shiva crossed the limits. How can he grant such a boon? Mahakaal is no more. No one else can now kill Kaalahar. How can this happen?

Lord Hanuman appeared into Swarglok and said, "Is this your intellect & wisdom? Is this what you have understood of The Mahadev (another name of Lord Shiva). Patience is the virtue. As of now, you have to follow what Kaalahar says. However, keep your trust in Mahadev; things never appear as they are. This is how his maya (play) is. Every such boon he gives is for better learning for each soul." After saying this, Hanuman vanished into air as usual.

Kaalahar and Guru Rakshit were happy. The whole Asura clan was celebrating. Guru Rakshit said to all "My friends, our time has come now. No one can stop us now. Let us make the whole world asuramay (filled with Asuras)."

Kaalahar went straight to Swarglok and expelled all Devas (Gods) from there. He took control of all Apsaras (beautiful dancers who serve Devas) and chaos began to be a member of Swarglok.

Kaalahar then unleashed 10 powerful Asuras of different Gunas (attributes) as Ahankara (Ego), Moha (Attachment), Krodha (Anger), Ghrina (Hatred), Bhaya (Fear), Matsar (Jealousy), Lobha (Greed), Kaama (Lust), Jadatva (Inertia/Insensitivity) and Mada (Pride). These asuras started grabbing minds of humans in every situation.

Humans failed to understand what was happening. Slowly, everything changed. Humans were strangled into these Asuras, captured completely.

Understanding Naam Shakti & Cosmic Frequency – Ram's realization

Indradev (king of gods and heaven) decided to attack Kaalahar. He forgot what Lord Hanuman had guided. All gods came together and gathered all the forces they could. Indradev, along with Agnidev (god of fire), Varundev (god of water), Vayudev (god of air) and their allied forces marched to Swarglok.

Kaalahar was expecting this, and so was his Guru, Rakshit. Kaalahar, as usual made his weird laugh and gathered all his forces.

A big war started like never before. Kaalahar came straight on Indradev. Indradev ran all over the places. From earth to moon, galaxy to galaxy, Kaalahar was just behind him.

Finally, Indradev opened his final Astra (weapon) that is Vajra. Vajra was the most powerful of weapons anyone could have in this universe. He had even used it successfully on Lord Hanuman when Hanuman was a baby. Kaalahar did not look afraid of it, though. Nonetheless, Indradev fired it onto Kaalahar. Kaalahar, no matter what, always used to chant Shiva's name in mind. He continued the same. The vajra hit him and just got merged into him.

"Wait, what is happening? Where is Vajra? Why it did not kill Kaalahar?" Indradev started thinking.

Suddenly Lord Hanuman appeared. He said "Indradev, how could you forget what I had told you? How can you even think that any weapon could kill that person who is protected by Lord Shiva himself? Especially when he has Shiva's name continuously in his mind with a boon that no one except Mahakaal can kill him.

Naam (i.e., name) is the key to realization. When the naam of a Lord encompasses a person's mind, body and soul, then that person does not remain a person anymore. He becomes one with God. Who can kill such a man?"

"But Lord Hanuman, Kaalahar is not a person. He is an Asura. Moreover, he's doing everything wrong, how can he be protected?" Indradev almost yelled.

Very calmly, Lord Hanuman said "Indradev, no matter who takes God's name; Asura, Sura, Deva, Human, Animal or even demons, the outcome is the same. It might take different time for each of them. But as long as the intensity and Bhakti of that being is high, God cannot turn a blind eye towards it."

Ram asked in-between to Gurushri, "What is the difference between chanting the name of God and chanting that name which is given by Guru in

NaamDeeksha (process in which Guru gives a secret spiritual name i.e., Naam to Shishya)?"

Gurushri replied, "You know now that how universe came into existence by one originating sound frequency and then slowly got manifested into different frequencies of energy and matter. Therefore, any soul which gets birth actually manifests itself with a specific frequency. This frequency is decided by that soul's learning purpose, karma and desires, etc. Now, god's name is one of the generic, high vibrating frequency names arranged in Sanskrit, which can bring slow and steady progress to anyone who chants it. It's a very simple and effective process. It slowly brings the person to a higher and higher frequency to eventually match the Universal originating frequency. However, when a Shishya (disciple) receives NaamDeeksha (Spiritual Naming Ceremony), it is the highest spiritual gift he receives from his Guru. People have forgotten importance and background of NaamDeeksha. They think it is just another name that Guru gives to his Shishya. But that is not the case. Guru and Shishya have a very special relation that no other two souls in this universe have. Guru liberates Shishya from this Maya and makes him aware of it. This is a job of no ordinary soul. So, for this purpose, Guru keeps examining his Shishyas for a very long duration. Only when he finds that the Shishya is fully dedicated and at right stage to move ahead, he imparts the NaamDeeksha.

How this is done is again a very beautiful process. Unlike god's name, which is very generic frequency sound for everyone, Guru actually refers to Shishya's soul, karmic background and learning purpose and finds out what is the missing frequency that needs to be added to Shishya's current frequency to match it with the Universal originating frequency. Therefore, compared to chanting just god's name, this chanting gives direct upgrade to highest required frequency. This ultimately gives enlightenment to the Shishya."

"But Gurushri, what happens with enlightenment? What is role of body after that if the enlightenment is for the soul?" Ram asked.

Gurushri answered with a smile "Ram, enlightenment and death are the same. The only difference between them is the awareness of soul when this happens. When the enlightenment happens, soul is fully aware of universal knowledge and consciousness and so logically, that person is, too. Therefore, the person, i.e., soul, can decide if he wants to continue his journey on Pruthvi Maya and probably help others, or take self-exit from this, which will be called as death anyways for other unaware people. In such death or such self-exit, kundalini rises to Sahasraar chakra. Union of kundalini, i.e., Shakti, happens with Shiva, i.e., the ultimate self, and further progress of soul starts by exiting the body. Death also happens in the same way, but in that case, it is Mahakaal who usually keeps account of this, creates situations almost six months prior to death and when time comes, brings the kundalini upward and allows soul to exit the body. Kundalini is the ultimate Shakti, so one should be very careful when doing meditations or activations related to Kundalini. There is another way some souls choose to attain enlightenment. That includes taking away the physical body, simply converting matter into energy again. It is to get merged into the light, i.e., Jyoti (The divine Light). Swami Ramalingam from Tamil area of India followed this path and merged into the light along with his body. His mantra

Arut Perum Jyoti, Arut Perum Jyoti

Thani Perum Karunai, Arut Perum Jyoti

Is a combination of such great frequency energy which gives faster and direct access to cosmic energy, and when ultimate time comes, allows the person to merge into the light."

Hanuman then said to Indradev, "Now you know your Ahamkar did not allow you to control or kill Kaalahar. It is not our duty to do so anyways. As per the boon granted by Lord Shiva, only Mahakaal himself can kill Kaalahar."

Hanuman then goes and attacks Kaalahar. He diverts Kaalahar, takes him into different galaxies, and keeps him busy.

Ram asked to Gurushri, "But how is this all related to me?"

Gurushri knew it was the right time. He asked Ram, "What was the boon Kaalahar asked for? It was to kill Mahakaal, and only Mahakaal could kill him. What Kaalahar forgot was that Vinash or killing somebody does not mean it is fully destroyed. The root energy gets transformed in such cases to base and such base energy, or what we call as soul, then travels from eighty-four lakhs (8.4 million) Yonis, i.e., species in layman language. Therefore, a soul travels, meaning it takes rebirths from one yoni to another to higher and higher level until it reaches to the human stage. Now if you see, Mahakaal never was killed, he just transformed his root energy to basic soul again just to respect the boon granted by Shiva to Kaalahar. The difference between a normal soul and soul of the entity such as Mahakaal is – when it reaches to Human form, it cannot die a normal death. Only a wish of death or act of death will merge its human body into five elements and release the soul back to its original state, i.e., Mahakaal in this case."

Anantadrishti stopped, and smiled with a gratitude on his face. He bowed down to Ram and was slowly merged into the void.

Ram did not understand it. He was just trying to understand what his Gurushri had said at the end.

Suddenly, the spark was triggered in his mind. Ram himself actually did not die. Ram was just acting to die and he actually became dead. The realization happens to him. He understands that he is nothing but Mahakaal.

Ram's soul was no more there. Mahakaal appears in front.

Kaalahar, who was sitting in his abode, gets to hear about this. By the time he starts thinking about what has happened, Mahakaal appears in front of him. A silence spreads all over the cosmos.

Kaalahar bows down and sits in front of Mahakaal and says, "Lord, I don't want to make the same mistake that Ravana did. Even when Lord Ram was in front of him, he was blinded by Maya. He could not see what was happening. I want to surrender myself to you and attain that wisdom which I missed earlier. I was blinded by desire to never die and had forgotten about the basic rules."

Mahakaal smiled and said, "Kaalahar, I cannot grant you any more life seeing what acts you have done in the cosmos. Nonetheless, like me, you will come back again and get a chance to have the supreme knowledge. Tathastu."

A stroke of sword, and a blissful peace spread across the cosmos.